The Scenic Loop: Davis Mountains State Park Highway

Larry Francell

Purple Feather Press · Texas

Printed in the United States of America

First Printing April 2023

ISBN 978-1-959600-03-9

Purple Feather Press

Georgetown, TX 78628

www.PurpleFeatherPress.com

The Scenic Loop: Davis Mountains State Park Highway

☥

On March 1, 1872, President U.S. Grant signed
legislation into law that created Yellowstone National
Park, thus beginning the public lands/public park
movement in the western United States. Yosemite,
Grand Canyon, Bryce and Zion canyons soon followed.
Almost fifty years before the Scottish engineer John
McAdam developed a process of combining broken stone
and tar or asphalt to cover roadways creating an all-
weather pavement. Public parks and economical
pavement were the origin of the Scenic Loop through
the Davis Mountains.

In 1880 the League of American Wheelmen was
formed by bicyclists requiring good roads for their sport.
Allied with this early "good roads" movement, which
was mostly centered in the West and California, over
100,000 bicyclists, challenged by dirt and gravel roads
and the antagonism of horsemen, wagon drivers and
pedestrians, joined the League. The Good Roads

movement and the League of American Wheelmen were instrumental in advancing the cause of adequately paved roads.

The first Good Roads Association in Texas was founded in 1903. The early efforts of the Association were directed at state government; the need for a highway commission, and legislation allowing state convict labor for road improvements. Although in the legislative session of 1907, the first speed limit was set at 18 miles an hour, this effort had little impact in Austin. Due to a lack of genuine progress the Association dissolved that year, this at a time when twenty states already had highway departments.

However, the automobile, even in Texas, could not be denied. Nationally, the number of automobiles was increasing exponentially. In 1900 there were 8,000 registered in the U.S., but by 1910 there were over 450,000 and by 1930 almost 23,000,000 were licensed. By 1925 almost a million were registered in Texas. America was truly discovering the freedom of the open road.

As they became more common in cities automobile clubs grew, mostly with an interest in improving county and intercity roads so driving was not limited to town limits. Texas A&M had already created a chair for highway engineering and, in 1910, in conjunction with the Texas Commercial Secretaries Association, the university sponsored a good roads meeting at the State Fair in Dallas. A new Good Roads Association was the result.

Photo by W.D. Smithers: Road to the Observatory

ϙ

By 1915 there were 126 local associations. Two years previous, the association had commissioned Robert Potts, Professor of Highway Engineering at A&M, to create a model bill for a Texas Highway Department. The bill passed the Legislature but was vetoed by Governor Oscar Colquitt. The legislation, as written by Potts, would have established a commission of five, two of whom were to be university engineering professors selected by the regents of A&M and the University of Texas. One of the reasons for Governor Colquitt's veto was his belief that professors should not use their time for non-instructional purposes.

By this second decade of the 20th Century and the ascension of the automobile, the creation and improvement of highways were now major national political and economic issues. In 1914 the Lincoln Highway, an amalgam of public and private roads and funds, became the first designated transcontinental highway running from Philadelphia to San Francisco. The first scenic road in American was the Columbia River Highway constructed between 1913 and 1922. This designated historic road runs from Portland to The Dalles in Oregon.

In this early period government involvement in road construction was hit or miss and, as one observer stated around 1910, "the highways of America are built chiefly of politics, whereas the proper material is crushed rock, or concrete." The Federal government finally began to subsidize and organize road construction with the Federal Highway Act of 1916, which authorized joint state-federal funding and cooperation.

Since no Federal funds would be allocated locally unless the state possessed, or created, a centralized highway agency, the State of Texas created the Texas Highway Department in 1917 in a bill signed by Governor James Ferguson on April 4. Texas became the forty-fifth state to create a highway department. In conjunction with the pass-through of Federal dollars, the enabling legislation authorized a state system of public roads and highways in cooperation with the various counties and under the direction of the Highway Department. In order to provide the state's required portion of allocated funds, the act removed automobile registration from the jurisdiction of the counties. The initial state fees were based on $.35 per engine horsepower with a minimum fee of $7.50. Commercial vehicles paid according to the weight carrying capacity of each wheel.

At the first public meeting at Mineral Wells, the Highway Commissioners announced plans for a statewide network that would consist of 8,865 miles of "improved roadways." In 1924 the State relieved the counties of their original maintenance responsibilities and required them only to furnish rights-of-way for new construction.

Meanwhile the rise of tourism and the public parks and recreational lands movement generated major increases in the national park system and was stimulating action in the individual states. As the automobile became the preferred alternative to railroads for vacation travel, new forms of western tourism began to emerge. As Americans took to the road in increasing numbers, parklands became a favored destination. The states, and even individual communities, discovered that tourism was potentially big business.

In response the Texas Legislature created the State Parks Board in 1923. However, the legislation did not provide funds for the actual purchase of land, and it was not until the early 1930s that they received limited authority to do so. The state parks movement finally gained momentum in 1933 through Federal aid in the form of New Deal programs such as the Work Projects Administration, Civilian Conservation Corps, and National Youth Authority. By 1941 there were 31 state parks in Texas.

Ŷ

The initial park movement in Texas, beginning in the 1890s and led primarily by the Daughters of the Republic of Texas, centered on monuments from the Revolution, especially the Alamo and San Jacinto. The costs of park acquisition and development slowed the process for reasons stated in 1925 by Governor Pat Neff, "when she entered the Union, she refused to surrender her public domain. Texas, however, has sold or given away practically all her public lands, aggregating 172 million acres. She did not reserve one beauty spot, nor set aside anywhere one acre of land to be used and enjoyed by the public in the name of the State." It was Governor Neff who fought for the creation of the State Parks Board.

As early as 1922 a group of boosters were urging the state government in Austin to create some type of park or preserve in the Davis Mountains. The leader of this group was Walter S. Miller of Fort Davis who managed the Limpia Hotel. Besides promoting a park for the mountains, Miller was instrumental in assisting the University of Texas in finding a location for McDonald Observatory. His son Keesey Miller stated that his father "spent a few thousand dollars, untold amounts of time, and wore out two automobiles" on these two projects. In 1933, as the land acquisition for an observatory on Mount Locke was taking place, Miller convinced the commissioners of Jeff Davis County to approve a preliminary survey for a road, a section of which would soon be the first portion of the Davis Mountains State Park Highway.

Photo by W.D. Smithers:
McDonald Observatory Dome under construction

In the spring 1927, in a flurry of activity to boost tourism, State Senator Thomas Bell of Dallas introduced a bill in the Texas Legislature instructing the Highway Department to develop the Davis Mountains State Park Highway through the heart of the mountains. This was at a time when most of the roads in Jeff Davis County were unpaved ranch roads. In

1928 the total expenditures for highway construction in the county was $1,880.90.

There was an initial appropriation of $10,000 for the project. The right-of-way, 150 feet wide, was to be donated by area landowners. Initially this created a complication with the land donation for McDonald Observatory. Violet Locke McIvor, who controlled the property, had already donated 200 acres of land to the state park project when approached by Mr. Miller to donate the land to the University of Texas. She eventually agreed to support both causes.

Senator Thomas Love, a major proponent of the project, estimated the total costs at $300,000.00. Love, a regular summer visitor, wrote. "Fort Davis is a mile high, the same altitude as Denver, where thousands of visitors go annually, and its climate is perfect. I have visited some of the greatest scenic places in American and Europe and there is nothing I have seen that exceeds the beauty and grandeur of the Davis Mountains." With the real possibility of a modern highway providing access, the land for the right of way was donated by twenty local ranchers.

Photo by W.D. Smithers:
McDonald Observatory Dome under construction

♀

In the same year, 1927, George Finley joined the Highway Department as a division engineer stationed in Alpine, retiring as head maintenance engineer in 1950. He recalled receiving his instructions from State Engineer Gibb Gilchrist, "a recent Legislature made an appropriation of $10,000 to cover the cost of the Jeff Davis Scenic Drive. This drive is to begin at Fort Davis, go out by the McDonald Observatory and then by the Rockpile Ranch and then by two camp meeting sites and back to Fort Davis for a distance of approximately 75 miles. I want you to go up there and go over this route very carefully and the write me if you think we should make this survey at this time."

Finley's reply is instructive of the difficulties, "well, there was no use for him to tell me to go over this route very carefully. That was the only way you could get over it because it was one pile of rock almost from one end to the other and if there was one gate, there must have been 25. These were wire gates and hard to open and harder to close."

Actual work on the road began on January 9, 1932 near the old Fort Davis pump house on Limpia Creek. Since the work was supervised by the Highway Department, no construction contract was let. Local labor and equipment were employed, initially using horse drawn fresnos and blades, as well as, much dynamite. In June Governor Ross Sterling made a personal inspection of the first fourteen miles of the completed road.

Even with legislation authorizing the construction, the development of the Davis Mountains State Park Highway was a hit and miss affair until 1933 when New Deal efforts and agencies began to play a role in the country's economic recovery. Early in 1933, Parks Board member Phebe Warner reported that, "tragic as the depression has been state park projects have thrived under it as the parks furnished an opportunity for public work." She continued to report that the Davis Mountains project was "being built by home people and almost entirely out of the materials on the ground."

Photo by W.D. Smithers: The town of Fort Davis

ϙ

Thus, it may have been native pride that prompted the Fort Davis Chamber of Commerce to hire the well-known regional photographer, Wilfred Dudley Smithers to document the Davis Mountains State Park Highway. Smithers (1895-1981) was born in San Luis Potosi, Mexico where his father was a bookkeeper for the American Mining and Smelting Company. In 1905 the family moved to San Antonio, but Smithers would always maintain his connection to Mexico, traveling and photographing there throughout his life. Smithers, never completing high school, had an early interest in photography and worked at various jobs while learning photography at a San Antonio studio. From 1915 to 1917, during the border troubles, Smithers worked as an Army teamster throughout the Big Bend.

In 1917, he enlisted in the U.S. Cavalry, but soon transferred to the Aviation Section of the Signal Corps where he could pursue his interests with aerial photography, including the recently developed gun camera. Discharged in 1919, Smithers operated a photographic studio in San Antonio from 1920 to 1929, often free-lancing as a photojournalist for various news organizations. In the 1930s he returned to the Big Bend, finally settling in Alpine. In the following decades he documented the Big Bend region, the U.S.– Mexican Border, and traveled and photographed extensively in Mexico. Overall, he created almost 10,000 images that he describes in his 1976 autobiography, *Chronicles of the Big Bend*, as follows, "my photography would direct itself to historic and transient subjects – vanishing lifestyles, primitive cultures, old faces and odd, unconventional professions. Before my camera I wanted huts, vendors, natural majesties, clothing, tools, children, old people, the ways of the border."

The Fort Davis Chamber of Commerce contracted with Smithers at a most opportune time. Concurrent with the State Park Highway, the University of Texas was constructing the dome for the 82-inch telescope and support structures, and the young men of the Civilian Conservation Corps were busy constructing Indian Lodge, the signature structure of the Davis Mountains State Park. Both of these major projects would figure prominently in Smithers' photo-documentation.

The Title Slide from W.D. Smithers'
documentation of the State Park Highway

When Smithers began the process of documenting the Davis Mountains State Park Highway, the road ended just beyond the observatory. Of Smithers' sixty images documenting the Scenic Loop, two-thirds were of this area – Fort Davis, Limpia Canyon, Davis Mountains State Park and Indian Lodge, McDonald Observatory, and the road leading to the top of Mount Locke. The second largest grouping of images are ten taken on the Merrill Ranch in the area of Point of Rocks close to Fort Davis where the road was yet to be constructed. Most of these are ranch scenes of cattle herds and working cowboys. The rest of the images are of Sawtooth Mountain, the Rockpile and Mount Livermore, all taken from the area of the Reynolds Rockpile Ranch.

Photo by W.D. Smithers: Sawtooth and Rockpile Ranch

To attract the widest possible audience to the Davis Mountains State Park Highway, Smithers produced his original images as lanternslides. Because the chemicals he had to work with produced only black and white images and he wanted to show off the Davis Mountains to the greatest possible effect, all 60 images were hand colored.

The *Magic Lantern*, as it was called, pre-dates the development of photography. It is a machine designed to cast a transparent image or drawing onto a flat screen. This lantern used a light source and magnifying lens to project an image many more times larger than the original – thus the name *magic lantern* for the magical quality of the images produced. The first transparent photographic images were produced in the 1850s, and by 1860 the Langenheim Brothers of Philadelphia were producing commercial lanternslides and machines.

Lanternslides reached their greatest popularity in the early 1900s, and were a favored method for illustrating public lectures and travelogues of exotic places. To make the images more dramatic the slides were often colored by hand-tinting. The quality and realism of these hand-tinted images were predicated upon the artistic ability and aesthetic sense of the colorist.

Lanternslides consist of a transparent positive photographic image sandwiched between plates of thin glass and bound around the edges by black paper tape. Often the photographic image is integral to one of the interior glass surfaces. These slides were of a standard size of 3¹/₄ by 4 inches. Beginning in the 1930s color films and the less fragile 35 mm slide replaced the lanternslide. Due to the lack of color density of the dyes used for tinting, lanternslides are difficult to copy. Modern computer scanning and digital color correction makes this task much easier.

Photo by W.D. Smithers:
Working Cattle on the Merrill Ranch

Photo by W.D. Smithers:
Indian Lodge under construction

The Davis Mountains State Park Highway, different from the soon to be created Davis Mountains State Park was, as originally designed, unique. It was to be a linear park or scenic driving parkway, not a park in the traditional sense. It was probably for this reason that the Davis Mountains State Park, nestled in Keesey Canyon and possessing one of the most unique hotels in the state, Indian Lodge, came to take priority over the scenic road.

Photo by W.D. Smithers: Scenic Overlook on Skyline Drive, Davis Mountains State Park, Built by the CCC

Construction on the roadway towards McDonald Observatory was well underway when Companies 879 and 881 of the Civilian Conservation Corps arrived in June 1933 to set up camp in Keesey Canyon. Company 881 departed in November of that year while Company

879 labored on until July 1935 working on campgrounds, support buildings and the Indian Lodge. The original furnishings were built by the CCC, but at Bastrop State Park, not locally. The architect Arthur Fehr, who did the major design work at Bastrop State Park, and his friend William Calhoun Caldwell took over the design of the Indian Lodge. The final touches were being applied when W.D. Smithers arrived with his camera.

The Civilian Conservation Corps Camp building the Davis Mountains State Park in Keesey Canyon

Besides the lodge and support buildings, the CCC was also constructing the Skyline Drive – a scenic road along the top of North Ridge Mountain adjoining the ruins of old Fort Davis. Smithers dutifully documented the stone overlook at the end of this loop.

Photo by W.D. Smithers:
View of Fort Davis from Sleeping Lion Mountain

While Davis Mountains State Park with its Skyline Drive took precedence in the public's mind, the State Park Highway continued to be important to tourism in Texas. In the Centennial year of 1936, the Legislature instructed the Highway Department to give priority to this project, "it is highly important that the thousands of Centennial visitors from other states shall have the opportunity of visiting and inspecting this great Texas Mountain Area."

In reality the entire Scenic Loop was not completed until after World War II. The road was formally dedicated and opened on June 28, 1947. This was twenty-one years after the initial effort began. The total costs were estimated to be $950,000, consisting of 75 miles of pavement looping through the heart of the Davis Mountains, beginning, and ending in Fort Davis.

A combination of State Highways 118 and 166, the Loop travels up Limpia Canyon on 118 past the entrance to Davis Mountains State Park and the historic Prude Ranch on its way to McDonald Observatory on Mount Locke. Today the observatory complex includes not one but three major domes and several minor ones, with the new Hobby-Eberley

Telescope dominating Mount Fowlkes on property
obtained by the University of Texas in 1933.

Photo by W.D. Smithers:
Indian Lodge under construction

The road to the top is a detour from the primary
Loop, which continues west into the high country. From
the highpoint of Fisher Hill, the road drops down into
Madera Canyon and a large roadside park, named for
Lawrence E. Wood. Wood, the highway engineer in Jeff
Davis County from 1932 until 1943, oversaw most of the
construction of the Scenic Loop. From there the road

climbs once again to a pass called Beef Pasture Gap and then to Nunn Hill where Highway 118 continues on to Kent and Interstate 10. At this junction the Scenic Loop, as Highway 166, turns south towards the Rockpile and Sawtooth Mountain and continues to the junction with Highway 505, the cutoff to Valentine. Here the road turns east past Barrel Springs the location of an early stagecoach station and on to Skillman Grove the site of the annual Bloys Campmeeting, founded in 1890. This place is named for Henry Skillman who had the mail contract to California in 1851. Once while camped at this site his party, including the famous scout Bigfoot Wallace, was attacked by Apache.

The Bloys Campmeeting at Skillman Grove

Presbyterian preacher William Bloys chose this location for the permanent site of the Campmeeting that bears his name. The road continues from there to the landmark and roadside park at Point of Rocks, 12 miles from the return to Fort Davis. As the road loops through the Davis Mountains on its 75-mile meander, the pivot point that draws the attention of the traveler is Mount Livermore, the highest point in the Davis

Mountains. It is named for Army Engineer William Roscoe Livermore who surveyed the area in 1880.

At the time World War II erupted in 1941, the Davis Mountains State Park Highway was still not complete. By the time the war was over, and American's began to travel again for pleasure, the Davis Mountains State Park and Indian Lodge were well established and the concept of a linear park through the mountains somehow slipped away. However, this did not mean that the road would not be finished. The final work was completed in 1947. However, it was no longer the State Park Highway and was now known as the Scenic Loop, the name used today.

On June 28, 1947, the Davis Mountains State Park Highway was finally dedicated after "twenty-one years of everlasting keeping after it on the part of local citizens, state officials and highway officials," as stated in the official program. The dedication took place at what is now the Lawrence Wood Rest Area, and the high school bands from Fort Davis and Marfa provided the music. The ceremony was broadcast live over KVLF radio from Alpine. Speeches were made and the ribbon cut by eighty-eight-year-old Anton Aggerman the last surviving soldier to serve at Fort Davis. The Fort Davis Veterans of Foreign Wars Post provided the meal.

The Dedication of the Scenic Loop, June 28, 1947,
The Lawrence Wood Rest Area, Madera Canyon.

ꝗ

In the 1970s the section of the Scenic Loop from Fort Davis to McDonald Observatory was "widened and improved," destroying a number of the old cottonwood trees and springs where the Loop begins along Limpia Creek. In 2000-2001 Highway 166 from Fort Davis past Point of Rocks and the Bloys Campmeeting to the Valentine cut-off at Highway 505 was the subject of "improvement." This work encompasses approximately 50% of the original State Park Highway. However, the most scenic portion and the section that is not a connector to or from any community is the other 50% of the road through the high country from the Valentine cut-off, Highway 505, to McDonald Observatory. This section remains as it was when constructed, with the added benefit of the landscape growing to the edge of the pavement.

Included in this unimproved and original part of the Scenic Loop is one of the most beautiful roadside picnic areas in Texas, the Lawrence E. Wood Rest Area in Madera Canyon. Wood was the local Highway Department engineer for many years at Fort Davis and was instrumental in finishing this road. This original site was owned by A.R. Eppenauer. Mr. Wood organized a trade for another parcel with Walter Miller, the early proponent of McDonald Observatory and the Scenic Loop. Mr. Miller then donated the land in Madera Canyon for this rest area, one of the gems of the contemporary Scenic Loop. The Texas Natural Conservancy sponsors and maintains a hiking trail that begins at this site.

Today the Davis Mountains Scenic Loop is listed in Texas *Monthly* and other national magazines as one of the best bicycle rides in the state. In the same manner, numerous motorcycle magazines have listed the Scenic Loop as one of the best rides in the state and country. Motorcyclists and bicyclists arrive almost every weekend in Fort Davis. Both are important to the economy of the community.

The Davis Mountains State Park Highway is one of those stories that was overtaken by time and circumstance but is important to the development of the lifestyle and economy of the region. W.D. Smithers' documentation of the road and at the precise time that both McDonald Observatory and the State Park were being built, is a priceless by product of the project. What is left of the original road is narrow, steep, curvy, and beautiful, and deserves to be maintained as originally intended, the Davis Mountains State Park Highway. It should be designated as a historic road for Texas.

Photo by W.D. Smithers:
Two Cowboys

A Note to Bicyclists:

Based on personal experience, the best way to ride and enjoy the Scenic Loop is clockwise. In this manner the first half of the ride is relatively flat and gives one time to acclimate. The first significant climb occurs at HO Canyon, about the halfway point. From there it is a gentle ride to Nunn Hill at the highway intersection to Kent. From the top of Nunn Hill, one follows the Cherry Creek drainage where the elevation begins to increase. At the top of Beef Pasture Gap there is a steep downhill past the entrance to the Texas Nature Conservancy's Davis Mountains Preserve ending at the Lawrence Wood Rest Area, a good place to take a break before attacking Fisher Hill, the steepest climb on the ride.

From the top of Fisher Hill to McDonald Observatory there are rolling hills with numerous gear changes. Past the observatory the fun begins, with a long, steep, and winding downhill that, at the bottom, culminates in a hill, that regardless of momentum, one cannot coast over. That's an important point: no matter how fast one is going geography will apply the brakes. The last few miles go past the historic Prude Ranch, the Davis Mountains State Park and back to town.

Riding the Loop in this manner one avoids the massive climb up Mount Locke to the Observatory in the first twelve miles of a seventy-five-mile ride and can enjoy an exhilarating downhill at the point when one begins to wonder, "why am I doing this."

Bibliography

Evans, David & J. Derral Mulholland. *Big and Bright: A History of the McDonald Observatory.* University of Texas Press, Austin 1986.

Golden Anniversary: Texas Highway Department, 1917-1967. Texas Highway Department, Austin, 1967.

Jacobson, Lucy Miller & Mildred Nored. *Jeff Davis County, Texas.* Fort Historical Society, 1993.

Smithers, W.D. *Chronicles of the Big Bend: A Photographic Memoir of Life on the Border.* Texas State Historical Association, Austin, 1999.

Steely, James Wright. *Parks for Texas: Enduring Landscapes of the New Deal.* University of Texas Press, Austin, 1999.

The New Handbook of Texas. Texas State Historical Association, Austin, 1996.

Author Bio

Larry Francell earned a Bachelor of Arts in History from Austin College and a Master of Arts in History from the University of Texas at Austin. He has worked for Texas Parks & Wildlife, and the National Park Service at Fort Davis National Historic Site. He spent many years in the museum business and was a partner in FAE Worldwide, an international museum and arts services company. In 1996 he sold his portion of the business to move to Fort Davis where he and his wife Beth purchased and restored her family home.

He has spent over twenty years in county government, is the author of *Fort Lancaster: Texas Frontier Sentinel; Planning for the Move of a Museum Collection; How Indian Emily Saved Fort Davis; What's in a Name: Why Fort Davis Was Named for Jefferson Davis and Why the Name Was Never Changed,* plus numerous articles on local history and museum operations. One of his personal goals is the recognition and preservation of the original and unimproved portion of the Davis Mountains State Park Highway.